Whispers

NORMA FREDRICKS

HybridGlobal
PUBLISHING

Published by
Hybrid Global Publishing
301 E 57th Street
4th Floor
New York, NY 10022

Manufactured in the United States of America, or in the United Kingdom when distributed elsewhere.

Fredricks, Norma.
Whispers
     ISBN: 978-1-957013-27-5
     eBook: 978-1-957013-28-2

Cover design by: Jan Shapiro
Copyediting by: Dea Gunning & Linda Fredricks Coghlan
Interior design by: Suba Murugan
Author photo by: Fred Fredricks

Dedication

This book is dedicated to Fred who helped write my life.

Table of Contents

Suddenly Summer

Summer comes suddenly,
Essentially intolerable and
vastly overrated.
A season of decisive heat,
of bare backed clothes,
and dampened sheets.
We skip through it on our
sweating feet,
and joy each year,
in its retreat.

Margo

There is no Margo in Key Largo
and not again in "Rain,"
Neither Hemingway nor Somerset
Chose to use the name.

It never struck their fancy
to name "Margo" their queen,
Nor could their lives be lengthened
to change a single scene.

But had they known this little one,
our Margo oh so sweet,
they would have altered all their words
and other names delete.

So, to Margo only, go her credits,
our applause and admiration,
To her grandma goes the special joy
of loving this new sensation.

Sunrise

The sun rose slowly at first
Peering across the rim of the land,
Shaking off the night.
Its rays, teasing and tentative,
spreading and growing
Waking the day
Guiding our way

The Kitten

A kitten sits watch outside my door
She guards the fortress that is my room
And there, she serves me well.

This tiny feline - this purring ball of fur,
Who never wants to go to places,
not concerned with her.

But she loves best, the role she plays
just outside my door
Where she remains my champion
the hero I adore.

There is a place within my heart
she always will remain -
I'll guard her there forever
within our shared domain.

A Child

A child, a wonderment
a lovely thing to see,
Fashioned of agile limbs
and boundless energy.
A child, a miracle - the greatest treasure
His smile more sweet
than countless flowers,
Loving to be loved.

A child. A blessing. A brand-new thought.
A free being to mold with greatest care
to fulfill the promise,
A child. A legacy.
Memory of what we were
and wish for him to be.
An enchanted gift,
we cherish.

The Party

It was the day after the party,
the lampshades drooped
and gala papers hung
as rumpled by a raging sea.

The tired but happy souls
who slept beneath the memories
of what occasioned such a day,
were still at rest
so as to strengthen,
for the cleaning up
of all their play.

"Twas fun, twas fun indeed.
But how many lessons do they need?
With the money it costs
And the havoc it wreaks,
Tis better not to throw a ball, at all!"

To Fred

Remember, dear when we were young
and lived away from all we knew?
Remember how we shared our world,
when all we had was me and you?

Later, life moved us in varied ways,
fortune changed and children grew,
I labored side by side with you,
and loved you more and more.

Sometimes by chance, and sometimes by plan,
the man you became and the woman I am
Walked hand in hand life's challenging road,
along that path, we have both grown old.

So I tell you now, my husband dear,
as sunsets race by and endings grow near,
I enjoyed being a woman, a mother, a wife,
I will love you forever,
as I have all my life.

The Daily News

I read your words
from page to page,
Absorbing much that is
the rage.
The trifles here
and nonsense there,
Your bold black headlines
fill with fear!
Is this a piece of worth you think?
That talks of dirt and crime in ink
as if to say, it happened, yes,
And happily before
We went to press.

A Child Grows

How grow you, child,
so tall and straight
Within our home, beneath your mother's gaze?
And how did the little hands I held
reach near man's size?

Those tender limbs I nestled once
Now carry books and cross the street,
and run and jump on great big feet.

Time, my baby, has made you taller,
while to you, my love,
we have just grown smaller.

Familiar Heart

Those hearts that beat

at pace of run,

to them a love, has just begun.

To them the world is full of joy,

the hope of the future,

in a girl and boy.

Beauty

A side of cream

softened and scented

A puff of oils

with perfume vented;

our skins reward

Why I Love My Mask

For most of a year, I haven't spent one dime on a new lipstick,
almost all of my face is protected by my mask.
Thus my mask provides me with some' monetary economy.

When I was very young, my favorite radio hero
Was The Lone Ranger.
His buddy referred to him as 'The Masked Man.'
He thus acquired an air of mystery under his mask,
an unnecessary disguise since we could not see him in
any case.

I brush my teeth less frequently
and hardly ever use a mouth wash (another savings of sorts).
I hardly converse with anyone except by phone.
My last fluffy haircut has turned to long and straight
and is held neatly in place by the stretch of ear cords of my mask.

My mask helps me avoid contact with the illness
that could curtail my life.
Wearing it is hardly the most difficult thing to do;
and everyone should!

During this dreadful period of time,
you too can learn to love your mask.
Soon we will be able to be together and hold each other,
place our masks in our drawers,
gone, but never forgotten.

Just Passing Through

I never stopped to think
of time,
or that I was just passing
through.
Only now, when my life is
ending,
and my time is coming due.

I suggest you learn to
enjoy the flowers,
Share your joys with
loved ones and friends.

Take time to see life's
beginnings,
And face life, when it
truly ends.

I recall my own
beginning,
when first I was a child,
later I became a sister,
then I became the bride.

My own life has passed
more quickly,
than while passing, it did seem
So many memories
exist today,
they remain part of
all my dreams.

Please be kind to
this world of strangers
who may not know it yet,
In this life we
share on earth
this is all the time we get
Because, my friends
here everything ends.

So enjoy your life
and celebrate,
be fair to all and be true.
Live life to the fullest,
remembering, we are
All just passing through.

So Little Kindness in Mankind

It seems to me
that life is sometimes cruel and hard
As watching, I observe the blows it deals
to those who least deserve.

Imperiled and alone,
with receipt of stone upon stone,
Time swoops down
to steal the old
and grind again the meek and bold.

The Man Who Should Not Be

A man who lies as swiftly as flood waters flow,
he drowns the sweeter grasses
where healthy flowers grow.

He feels no shame and takes no blame
for the evil he is doing,
He smiles and he pretends
it's not all of us he's screwing.

Coarse and cursing, mouth like a sewer,
he salutes the US flag,
but prefers a foreign ruler!
Americans made him their President,
for which there is not precedent.
So vote him out and turn him over
(I for one will be in clover)
Ring the bell, fill the well,
and tell the man to go to Hell!

The Liar's Party

(Motto: "Goodbye to Truth")
To grow this 'party,' we need only disguise
The mountain of lies that
spout from the mouth of our leader!
Now we all know the rules, having mastered the tools,
for spreading false lies to America's fools.

We say, no matter the shame, our big lies work
and our small ones take aim.

We have long been planting the seeds,
and performing the deeds, that will assure,
our party of hate succeeds!
So, watch our Democracy start shrinking,
as our party keeps linking
to hate groups of multiple sorts.

This nation is ours, since the truth left the gate.
So keep up the big lies, keep spreading the hate.
Remember the damage we caused when the 'help came too late!
Lies can conquer all,
This is our fate!
Heil! Trump!

Vote 1

I so lament and hold in contempt,
the man who was our President.
His true believers impress me not,
I've seen this all before.

When Hitler called,
they followed him,
This man is like the other.

He will sell us out with evil lies,
and thus provide a sequel,
Create a world – where lies are truth,
in this he has no equal.

This man, who from his very start,
Grew up without a caring heart.
His brain from greed,
will not be parted.
He never learned to be kind-hearted.

He acts upon his every whim,
no pain to others troubles him,
No charity of soul exists.

Vote 1 (continued)

He studies nothing
and absorbs much less,
He played too long,
in the sand I guess.

If we could but see him without a slanted edge,
we would know he's not a normal man,
Just one who's standing on the ledge.

Deliver us from this evil man,
restore us to a healthy nation-
Stop him and all his evil lies,
let truth be our salvation!

Victory, 2020

My heart is beating slower,
as my anxiety relents.
I'm glad so many people
showed such good sense.

Biden is the new man,
our future President.
He will soon put an end
to a foul Washington scent!

Please go, Mr. Trump, show a
bit of good grace.
We are really sick of your liar's face.
Get over your loss,
you are no longer the boss.
You're fired!!!

Night

The night takes a full possession
of the sky
The stars dance
and the moon glows
brightly colored in a darkened world.
The comfort born of sun and light
that is by day
has truly vanished
In this dark reflection, the sky does shield
us better, from the earth
on which we live.
The loneliness we feel deep within our roots
we share with this planet, adrift
amidst a sea of distant lights
Till the morning waves a sunlit banner
and wearies of the silence here,
We have nothing save the sleep that comes
to shield our shivering souls.
When dreams depart and black
night retreats,
We may dip our famished spirit into
a store of hopes,
Replenish our souls as to pass another day,
in search of love and life's meaning...

Young Charles of All My Dreams

Come say hello and sing with me.
Make happy sounds that charm the birds.
I will hear your music and your words will make me smile.
When you awaken and the day is new,
all about will stir to be with you.

When night webs clear and my mind's alert,
I'll think of all you'll do
To move the world,
and I will smile.
So play gently with your happy style
Such sweetness charms the ones you love.

Beloved child, much loved child,
The "Charles" of all my dreams.
When day is through and stories read,
kisses blown and sleep comes near,
Will you know that I am smiling dear,
And loving you?

My Dear and Darling Daughter

Always, as she arrives,
I feel her warmth.
Perhaps it is the glow
she presents with her loveliness.
Her affection comforts me
and fills me with grateful love.

My sweet child
is a strong tree to me,
a tree with tender branches
reminding me of other seasons.

My dear and darling daughter
makes provision for my heart,
she restores joy to my life
and nourishes my content.

A Story of John

He came to us, a stranger then,
a slender man with sharp blue eyes,
His voice with an accent of a different king,
and asked of us in an old fashioned manner,
a question for a parent's ear.

He asked us for Linda's hand in marriage,
and told us then, "my love is there where Linda stands,
I want her for my bride to be,
I want her for my life, you see."

He asked us if his question pleased us both,
as asking had so pleasured him.
And so it came about that a marriage followed
swiftly here.
Wife and husband, husband and wife,
together always for all of their lives.

So many moments to make a day,
so many hours, flyaway,
Dreams are shattered and the world turns grey.
Sadly, John's life was not to be,
illness stole his time away.

A Story of John (continued)

When springtime came,
his health retreated
And lovers prepared to say goodbyes.

We said farewell to our young man
With broken hearts we closed our books
on all our dreams and
what might have been.

Now he is gone,
we stand enriched,
by his having been ours,
lonely for him, always…

Our Friend's 50th Anniversary

It is very clear
that your love affair
has lasted long indeed,
We're really quite impressed
with how well
you did succeed.

It speaks of gentle understanding,
of kindness and good will,
a marriage made of many dreams
that lasts and lingers still.

We celebrate your fifty years
and truly honor you,
with wishes for your health and joy,
from friends both old and new.

May you always walk together
and your love continue on,
your days be like a blessing
throughout the years to come.

Gossip

Keen senses kindled
sharp as spruce,
acid tendered, twisted truths,
pepper scented, stale, fermented.
The old witch gossip, harshly vented.

Bitter bargain, wrestled course and smart,
precisely vented, in equal part.
Violet shaded, death paraded
the cruel tongue wags,
with mind unaided.

Love's Source

Beneath all this, an unknown truth lies, unyielding,
in fine, soft growths of pleasures, secrets stored.
Refusing in such sweetness born,
to answer all to me.

My brain, benumbed by this emotion
cast upon my weakened limbs.
I can do no more
than bend to all the burning need of this.

Unable to define the source,
to know only that I love,
and that you are my beloved.

Going Slow

I cannot remember all the
things I know
Nor forget the dreams I had with you,
so many facts have been forgotten,
I must assume this old brain
is rotting.

I once was great with names and figures
but now I cannot withstand
the rigors
of remembering.

So sound me out and learn from me
that which I still recall,
for very soon, my friends,
I may not remember,
a single thing at all!

Bon Voyage, Myana

Skip to the light fantastic
and visit every hallowed hall,
Sail your ship as if the master
Thus, my dear,
you'll have a ball.

Myana

She will first ride a train,
and then board a plane,
to reach a long river
that smacks of Mark Twain.
Then board a steamship
on which she will sail,
where so many joys
will likely prevail.
Remember that friends
await your return,
there is much you can give us
and much we can learn.

Dear Friends

I recall the many friends I had,
and how seeing them again
would make me glad.

They were not all pretty
but all were quite smart,
Each held a special place
in my heart.

I am no longer one
of that feminine crew,
As the last one is gone,
of the ladies I knew.

We may soon be together
as my life nears its end,
I will be joining them soon,
as the last of the friends.

We will rejoice and surrender,
hold loved ones so tight,
Dance in the darkness
and play in the light.

Dear Friends (continued)

Each friendship is precious
and in a lifetime, so few,
Now they are all waiting for me,
and I will be waiting for you.

Seasons

The snowflakes fall,
original and brief
A flowers face will fade
with the autumns' leaf
as seasons change.

Winter

The winter covers all
with pure white drifts of snow,
And buries in an icy grave
the sands and stones
That later, in a final season,
cover all of us.

Setting Sun

The sun is setting
on an old life lived,
now beyond usefulness and unloved.
Only tears can spend our later strength
and while flowing,
ease our empty shells
so that we may know
we are still alive.

Whispers

Whispers are the unspoken
words I write for you,
silent words, floating on
a tranquil sea.

They are my special thoughts
I choose to share with you,
so that you might best
remember me.

These whispers of mine will soon be ended,
and my pen will soon be still,
no more will my words be rendered,
as I have grown old
and lost the will.

Now you must record your
own whispers,
put your very best thoughts to pen.
Recall those who have gone
before you
and think of them
once again.

Know that I have loved you
very dearly and true
Search my very best whispers,
Where there remains
my loving memories
of you.

Regrets

Oh, the songs we could have sung,
the words we should have spoken,
the promises we kept,
and others that were broken.

We had so little time to wonder
why so many dreams just passed us by.
Now loves of old are dead and gone,
Their lusts resolved and passions done,
swept by time that fades us all,
I weep for those who loved us well,
and hold more dear what still remains.

The sky, the land, the children that I love,
without the man who nurtures me,
I too would be no more!

A Later Season

A new season has arrived
a swifter father time
presses on with life.

It is to be my final season
I feel much anger at having grown this old
at not having been more attentive to the passing years.

I am like the dried yellow leaves in the late autumn light
Goodbye to old lives and young beauty.
I'm free to be no more.

Friendship - To Bob

It pleasures us at this year's
end,
so loving a fellow to count
our friend.
No goods have we, no treasures
rare,
Nor friendship that we
hold more dear.

Time

The day's pass slowly
into night
When all goes wrong
and naught goes right.
When some joys come
into view
time will move by,
Two by two…

Another Place

There are no places to
which we go
that are so final.
No spaces that are so
permanent,
As the ground we will occupy
when death descends
and all things end.

The Clouds

The tops of trees
brush the clouds away,
and leave behind
blue slate on which to write
a better day…

Set in Stone

Set in this, oh, so unhappy environment
I am like sand cast into stone,
solidifying in my stupor,
non-engaged and hardening!

Alive only in the memories of
having lived,
revealed in furious flashes
of light and darkness.

Loves Distance Lost

Oh, my love -
how hard it is
to pass this day,
with you so close
and me so far away.

This Old Face

I am dancing very slowly,
on this familiar ground,
to the beating of drums
that produce no sound.
This very old face,
now like wrinkled lace,
is soon doomed to lose
life's ancient race.
Alongside a hidden stream,
one that flows,
then dies,
there, shall I, beneath
the fallen lilies lie.

Horror

His pain is what I see.
My pity and my sadness
overwhelm me!

If the clouds were black
and storm showers fell
that day, this tale
would better tell.

But the day is bright
and the air is sweet.
While my love lies dying
in the sunlight of our defeat.

Silence

He cries aloud, and yet
remains unheard.
His meaning hidden in his
soundless words.
His message is lost to all
but me.
A silent world of unintentional
censure,
An aged chorus of revolt.

Life is a Death Sentence

Preceded by many types of related body failures,
frequently accompanied by pain.
The good times have vanished
except for those stored in memory
or recalled by photos viewed in dusty albums.

Life was a better place in youth,
a time of exploration
now regrets replace old dreams
and I am left joyless
in nothingness.

Book Ends

It is simply a matter of printing this data
and sending it out to a friend.
Then everything new can come into view
and my poems can come to an end.

About the author

I grew up in New York City when street games were the major form of entertainment. Girls jumped rope and boys played stick-ball. Occasionally, we all joined for a lengthy game of Hide and Seek.

Indoors, books from my neighborhood library occupied my time. I was a good student and Valedictorian in Junior high and High school. Then I met Fred! Our marriage lasted 60 years.

Our first two years were spent in Europe, each at the courtesy of the U.S. Army.

Our children, Jack and Linda gathered these poems, encouraging me to produce this little book. I am grateful to them. These whispers were intended only for them, now I am happy to share them with you.

www.ingramcontent.com/pod-product-compliance
Lightning Source LLC
Chambersburg PA
CBHW070944120626
46546CB00004B/1549